D1707387

CSU Poetry Series LXV

Cleveland State University Poetry Center

Acknowledgments

General acknowledgement is made to the editors of the following publications, in which some of these poems first appeared, sometimes in slightly different form: *Crazyhorse*, *KARAMU*, *HazMat Review*, *GSU Review*.

Special thanks to Norman, David, Matt, Mandy, Eric, Sarah, and Josh.

The author is grateful to the MacDowell Colony for supporting this work.

Published by Cleveland State University Poetry Center
Department of English
2121 Euclid Avenue
Cleveland, OH 44115-2214

ISBN: 1-880834-68-5

Library of Congress Catalog
Card Number: 2005932957

Ohio Arts Council

A STATE AGENCY THAT SUPPORTS
PUBLIC PROGRAMS
IN THE ARTS 40 Years

The Small Mystery of Lapses

Poems by Christopher Burawa

The Small Mystery of Lapses

Contents

for Christina

Now I live here, another island,
that doesn't seem like one, but who decides?
My blood was full of them; my brain
bred islands.

—*Elizabeth Bishop*

Shriven, of the Apothecary of Lies

I have buried my father for the fifth time.
Each pit more difficult to dig,
shallower than the last—the pines thick,
the going narrow, the loam
unforgiving as a heart.

So I quartered him as I had to,
trussed him over
like a bagworm.

Then stumbled upon a deer glade,
a ground of compounded shale,
bedded weeds.
I clear it all away.
The spade rips through the clinging
moss into a canary-gray loess. Exposed,
it curls into vellum scrolls.

How will this cover him?

But on them, written in a child's scribble,
are the notes to your daydreams.
Of course, I had to pry.
I hack and read and rest often.
Stacking a woodpile of Mesopotamian clay.

You had written,
"For five dollars, I'll tell you more."
And as I search my wallet, a roost of magpies,
who have only creaking pines to mime,
begin their cries ...

Then it happens—
through the branches
floats the cast pollen of paper birch.
A random, seeking, and rampaging sex,
a forest's sex, yet somehow patient.
This lint moves easily, dodges the spindled leaves.

What could I call it, a gentle school or swarm?
I don't know.
The shout must have been building
for weeks.

—*for Chris Offutt*

A Substitute for Birds During War

I once saw a three-legged pointer
running after children
through a difficult field
of blunted autumn stubble.

It holds a folded bird,
a waterlogged branch
in its mouth,
dropped every time the children
scatter bobwhites, jigging after
their aiming fingers and pow pows.

The dog pivots on its one back leg,
looking for a bird,
the severed flight, tumbling
like a Turkish thief's hand
propelled by the quick, clean
chop toward the crowd.

The begums screaming like wheat rust ...

It may never be found.

The children leave the dog behind.
It wanders in circles, emphatic
nose skimming over even
that decaying stick, searching
for a memory that flaps and bleeds.

I throw a stone for it to find.

The dog's tail scribbles in sky
"thrive, thrive."

Love's Burning Boy

—to L.C.

I've slowly set the table below a cabbaged shadow of oaks.
The field of rye wheat believes it's the sun,
a circling hawk obliges as moon.

"You will surely get to heaven, right?"
asks the bantam rooster.
It tips its head, one eye on the hawk,
the other on the lookout for an innocent bug.

I'll quote from the amateur beekeeper's manual:
"If the smoke-gun becomes clogged, relax."
But we don't—
because the rice pot hisses from the house.

We say instead, "I've got to eat that."

Spilling into the Nightfall of Its Belly

I've decided to repeat to you
what I've convinced myself of:
that this blue-and-white plate
is better than any I've ever eaten from.

Look, on the pearl and yellow salt lick
a barn swallow opens its spindle-barbed beak
into the intentional smile of its kind,
in a pause from hawking the pasture.

A cow dips to its knees.

Since that day when I mourned
the childhood campfire,
its many tongues,
I've known the midtown lake
was always frozen,
and from my window I watched
its ducks walk back and forth
from their islands
slowly to the feeding place—

the armless figures hurrying by.

Feeding the Flint: A Fugue

Blessed is he who called the flint
the student of running water.
                    —*Osip Mandelstam*

1. Evening, without suspecting

the horrors
Nero's nephew played, an obsidian
blade, a gift, down the wet nurse's cheek
while the first sticky smells of softwoods
sashayed in from between the stark legs
of the purple-armed Hermes. The emperor
couldn't help but think of bundled feet,
pure and white, and by most accounts,
clean. He often dreamed about inspecting
every young boy brought down from the Tyrol,
personally removing each warm grass shoe,
tossing it over his shoulder onto a growing heap
once the insides cooled. How later that night,
alone, he'd light the stack with hawthorn
and smile as the hay pipes whistled
and flames rose up to flap, to warm
his evening bath.

2. That Wish Only to Be the Flame

Why most citizens referred to him as
the Good Lazlo? He thought of himself
as the Gentle Muzhik. Both are lies
of degree, like his uncle's return
from the Byzantine,
after prospering, just so he
could sit below the almond trees,
accepting visitors detailed with fleas.

Lazlo arranges the homecoming, a greeting
of sorts, by posing the priest's head,
occipital bone cracked so it would not loll
on the offertory dish,
in the center of the bishop's writing table.

He lights beeswax tapers,
arrays the beard to hang down,
into space.

Is the sum of light a mouth moving a whisper?
So tempting to lean in and say, *You wanted to come
but now you cry into your beard*, jeweled
with nutshells.

Lazlo lays filigrees of oat honey
over the brow
and down, connecting the shells
to a table leg, cedar shift,

before trailing what's left
to the dry ants
in the iris bed introducing
the red lacquered door.

3. Before the Three-men-on-a-match Rule

The French soldiers bring their pipes.
War is hell on a pipe,
which must be allowed to dry,
be docked
for at least a day.

Every other day, the soldiers
roll loosened roped tobacco
between shaved edges of maps.

Our world becomes a field this way ...

With matches scarce,
the first man builds up the lazy spark
so that the second only
has to tug
a few times.

The fire for the third
now stretches,
licks at a thumbnail ...

I crouch into the scope
and let fly
spring's first bee,
for me—in the oak trees
the French are now inhaling—
a failing flame that resembles
the sleepy eye of leisure.

4. Just as pollen fills a lily's throat

and wood smoke last night's dream,
I will do as you say.

The bridge is twelve ...

You burn your numbered barns,
shoo the rats toward the town,
I will do as you demand, and wait
until the span seems like a field of blown
winter wheat, wave the torch
three times, light

the fuses and braids of old hay ...

And they'll climb and leap
from me, until we become the towers,
in a blind blossom dance.

Your joyful cries, indistinguishable
from the whoop of flame
that spins me,
will be, as you say,
punishment enough.

5. How to Survive a Forest Fire

In the rain, rain from the east,
Sabbath rain, the smudge of May,
the houses ignite—

and it's true, the calamity of storm
reduces the land a layer or two,
while in our throats, we gather,

stand in the path of the advance,
aching like the starving
deer bound by us by what we believe
is our unspeakable secret:

how we complicate even an empty grief
with salt.

6. And the Sea, a Song Doth Sing

Four months on, one week off,
is fine until the winter trawling
when we ply endless circles across poor Arctic
maps for the red fish
who apparently never sleeps,
anti-freeze through its veins.

You tell the cook you can taste it
no matter how he prepares the dish ...

Predict a wave,
toss the plate his way.

Four hours on, four hours off,

and sleep happens only when
you least expect it,
one bad movie after another—
the captain's wife's favorites.

The perpetual smell of cooking grease,
painted into the walls, ruins
the simple pleasure of a just baked
rye.

You play the Zippo across your palm,
stare at us eating. We know

you are now murdering everyone you love.
We know when the pain reflex dies,
so has our certainty
that we ever needed the sun.

A Wound Seen To

I must be dead
because the blow flies are bent on me.

Yet, the reddened and rubbed rope
I use to hang the yearly elk
rusts

like an aspergillum
riotous and addicted

ever since distance was measured
in chicken steps.

But I've broken no one's back here.

So let me wrap your wish
in this oak leaf.

It may grow.

What I know is, you'll never hear the clock tick
until we stop talking.

What Jarrell and I Have in Common

I lost all my scabs in public pools,
believing whole-heartedly in the properties
of chlorine.

A soft white membrane
that overnight becomes an opaque drum,
which will curl from the edges
as it heals, around the exact center of
the wound.

A basalt stone, compromised by rain,
sudden cold and thaws,
can slowly crease
around its core, leaving successive rings,
even a heart.

A stone you pick up by chance
splits apart, and within it,
a face.
The resemblance is long on you—so that this event

is like a mystery or miracle you don't want to over think,
because we all know a discarded
persona when we stumble over one. And what's more,

you have the proof—
patches of yellowing amaranths
creeping down the flinty basin—a version of heaven
that borrows your body, bursting skin.

II

Fishing at the Asylum

Imagine a night so dark
snow would make it worse.
Low, fleshy nimbus clouds,
a river above a river,
means wind, swirling snow,
snow to make you tired
or angry,
flakes that make you flinch
and follow.   Freud knows nothing of clouds ...

The car's headlights brighten against the old
asylum, painted a white meant to dull
even snow, a beacon, maybe,
it's hard to say, except that down
that long lawn is a fishing hole,
where, out of our superstition,
I used to stand and wave
back toward the building
while my uncle fished.   ... or fish.

The French nuns wanted a building
in the sign of the cross.
Drawings didn't help.   They locked the doors
What they got, instead, was a train station.   in tender ways.

My first time there, predawn,
only five patients still lived on.
I looked in the windows,
the salt-glazed glass
reflected variations of blue,
of a waterfall pool where trout   He doesn't believe me when I tell him
recover in the blur.   death *is* a cure.

19

I stop the car, pull on waders,
walk out until I'm almost swept
away, and cast.
I reel in the river with just a fly.

A trout strikes
and I'm not pulling, it's leaping.
The fish flies over my head,
its belly the pink of day,   In its mind,
with night bending at its back.   the trout will fight you to the death.

I remember to wave.

My Early Conscription

Even before summer we'd march
half a day to the wartime rummage
of an old north Atlantic lookout post,
a Quonset hut made a hay barn,
just to play in the graying attaché car,
last parked on a cliff's edge, facing the sea.

We'd bounce in the seats,
my older cousin always at the wheel, me
in the back, the buffeted courier,
wounded in twelve places
and with an urgent order in my head.

Today, a cloud flaps a black wing.
On a day like this I was alone,
and tried to play the driver, yelling
over my shoulder at the wounded man
to hang in there, for Christ's sake.
I heard the hiss of his parka
as he died—the wall of oncoming rain.

I checked behind the cracking leather seats,
for his dog tags, and found a billfold instead,
long and narrow buckskin,
cherubs trumpeting at the corners
of what might be blood spatter.
It had a smell of sitting water, and was as cool.
I skimmed it for money, found none,
seal it away in the coffee-can-of-finds.

It now sits on a sill,
streaked with an albumen of rust,
and has the red glow of those taiga ponds
surrounded by snow, the sacrificial bogs

revered because they never freeze.

I nod and nap in my chair
while the pines make the sound of
the slow drive-bys of insomniacs
on narrow wet streets ...

In my dream I am opening the wallet; it squeaks.
A picture of my father in uniform,
with another woman, is glued behind
a milky eye of mold. They are seated
at a table, clinking champagne glasses in a toast.
The flash has rendered the room behind them black,
while it blares their happiness. She looks at him
like he's won a war. He looks like I've never seen him
before, the ear-to-ear smile
of a first-kill matador.

This is the woman, I know from my mother,
who, she says, wanted to marry him,
give him a flat ruby
ring—in Iceland, the marriage stone.

I can hear myself in the room making the same 'ems'
of my mother's dreams, long moans
of meaninglessness.
I'm remembering the scar on his forehead,
a gash from hitting the wall in his car,
a story about an all night drunk, the weaving
back before reveille, a buddy or someone dead ...

I kick to wake up or stop the car
because the urgent order,
the only one I always had to deliver, was
send help.

Photograph by a French Tourist

The Original (1" x 1")
Three old men
stand in full or mid blink
and rubber boots.
They think they are standing straight
but lean where their heads go.
Two hold shovels like oars;
the other holds a turf spade.
They stand apart
as if two men
are missing.

The Blow-up
His left mittened hand holds the spade grip.
His right a fist, in which the bowl of a burl pipe
smolders, the black stem with a worn-whitened
tip, aims dowser-like down
the hard-scrabble street, where a farmer
walks at the head of his horse
drawing the two-wheeled dung cart,
and pedestrians walk
close to the buildings, and my great aunt
Soffia and her married lover
emerge from a house—

his head turned in a complicated moment.
She wears a sequined flapper hat.
Her dress frays the overcoat.
The famous red snail curl
secured to her forehead
with spit a given.
A man walking the opposite way,

across the street and parallel,
may be walking into a wall.

She is raising a blurry hand to her mouth
to stop a cough—
the cough of their undoing.

Rimbaud's Last Fever

O ye ants, get into your habitations, lest Solomon and his hosts
crush you (under foot) without knowing it.
                                        —An-Nami 27:18

Above Harar pages from British newspapers circle
—white wings against a star becoming sky—
until they reach the height of wind
where they turn again
and glide away
to drown in the Red Sea.

Like people, a place can have a twin.
A town, I'm certain, has a double,
a replica in the spirit of opposites.

Harar twins Charleville.

Skins ruin in the heat,
where the manure waits
for spreading.
Each dog's territory seems to begin
here. The result is somehow sardines.

The muezzin's call lifts me to him,
and in half light I see a leopard,
gorged on puppies, crawling on its belly
out of town.

The cat leaves a spoor no one will follow.

It is said you can't return to town
unless you stumble into it
elsewhere. Then everything

is familiar, as if an overlay
has been carefully taped to the corners.

Heat shivers

banana clumps in the cherry trees.
A caravan trail cuts through the kitchen.
Aluminum pots, lashed to a camel's flanks,
clank louder at this spot
between the volley of mortars.

Mother stands by the stove
without knowing why, feels she needs air, and
steps outside.

A rutabaga goes missing from the stock pot.

This alone explains the small mystery of lapses—
dry cough behind the front door,
a stuck door,
cold knob
—when she returns.

So here I live among the altered pigeons
who thrash their beaks looking for something
they remember as bread.
They dodge what I toss among the acacia pods,
step around what they think are rocks.

The finches remember.

In their new colors I fly with the goods
to perch and eat on the termites' white columns.

The crumbs lure Solomon's flat ants.

The inevitable war will produce no dust.

How David's son laughed
when the ants dropped their breakfasts
in alarm
at the approaching armies.

The king knew them as God knows us.
And so it goes.

The way the writing could end there
but had always existed here.
Invoices
turn into details of death ...

I observe a Danlik child wearing a bishop's ruby ring on its thumb

But my right leg lives in neither place—
unlike my left shoulder, in Paris,
now the possession of an azure-painted woman,
moonlighting as a seal skinner's
deft and nimble shadow.
The leg, swollen to the stitching,
has become a Yangtze carp.

In my sleep the fish rakes me along a river's bottom.
I cannot twist to see.

The water temperature drops.
We have left the diving ducks behind.

I pass into
roaring shadow.
Without pause,
I recognize all sound as laughter.

Skeletons of Spirits

People simply disappeared: whole road crews,
a traveler crossing between two known points,
a child with wet socks.

The family waits,
years pass, and one day
the priest shows up at the door.
The mother cries, beginning
a planting in air.

This is how a Reykjavik cemetery
became a park.

Stone walls gave it
an appearance of limits.
Wealthy burghers built two-story houses
nearby, bringing sidewalks with them.
Then the complaints to the city
of headstones too bright below a moon.
Cement pickets added to a wall,
in circumspect, the greening trees must fall.

Moss everywhere.

Now, few remember the park as burial ground,
or even a field, or horses and sheep
ripping its grasses.

On any day, the headstones disappear
into particular fall mornings—
made dim by the linked arms
of memorial birches,

the city's first inconsolable forest.

* * *

The noon cat rolls a tongue down
its matted back, opposite
an old man
in an olive tweed suit
and matching hat.

Magnus comes here to sit
and remember his only brother, Lofti,
who walked into a Canadian wilderness
fifty years ago. *Presumed dead*,
the official form still says.

The mother buried her favorite
photograph of him
inside an expensive cherry box,
somewhere behind the bench.

The noon cat has the wisdom of extra toes,
and couldn't care less about these facts, grooming
with the collected scent of evening.

A passerby would see Magnus
sitting as if in a daze of good bread,
or in jealous dream—of him standing
on the stern of an immigrant steamer,
looking up at the clouds

instead of the shore.
He'll never return or write.
But the vision ends
without funeral or inlaid box.
Magnus grieves for this self,
just as the noon cat leaves.
Now the future wakes,
to cull the likely conclusions of a day.

Because he believes
in punishment,
heaven, he thinks, must have no past.

       * * *

Magnus, the defender of the bequeathed fictions
of what lies below the vegetable gardens,
was without comment
when scientists upearthed
retaining walls of a Viking long-house.

He slurps spiked coffee
thinking of the summer birds
in the soil, unseen,
visitors who stay.
Never mind the round felt
mouse whose burrow collapses
from the weight of grazing horses.
But over the wall,

the ruin of a house dries in the open air.
In the window, Magnus sees reflected

a face smeared with the ritual oils of burnt sheep.
The daughter's pleas marked across the brow,
the wife's down the cheeks.

How should we mourn these missing?

This when Magnus has seen ducks swim
despite their grief,
sifting through the lake grass
after black-backed gulls quaffed their young.

The bony pellets dropped
remotely from the lake.

But what if, by some magic,
one survived digestion,
and more importantly
the fall,
and reappears flightless,
addled in the eyes

but neatly there,
ready to continue
the initiation, but
with a whole hood of stars unprepared?

And the nearly eaten bird
among the speckled rock:

it yawns but cannot sleep.

        * * *

It was found just where it was named,

had an east facing view,
no windows to speak of.

The missing door was his death pallet,
it seems.
What is certain:
some sheep were reduced to ash,
the slaves divvied up in the rain.
The unlikely saga continues from this point to say
the dead man's overcast horse wore
moss above gray,
wandered off on its own
as the burial ship wagged and burned.

Such were the horses then.

Just over a tin wall from the site,
in a small backyard
where the latecomer French once housed their women,

weeds grow through last season's
brittle heatherbrae.

During the first three days of new growth,
Old Magnus would remark how the bordering trees waved

like confirmed bachelors without curtains.

* * *

His brother comes to him in a dream of Saskatchewan,
where three men track a bull elk along a river.
The water frozen in thin sheets
and then the river dropping. Its run is silent. But
magnified with movement, makes the last man, his brother,
feel as if they've made no gain at all.
A fog slides with them. Upriver.
The views are brief, not hopeful, so they walk with heads
down, follow the black blood smearing onto
their snow-caked boots.

His brother's shoulders hunch
at a cry of a bird?

The men bungle the guns as they walk
up to the head of the gut-shot elk.
It rattles the ice from its beard,
as one man raises his gun. Then,

a bear drops on him from a tree.

Another fires his rifle into air.
Lofti drops his and runs
down the embankment to the river.
His first step breaks through to the water.
The ice is at his thigh.
He eases below the shelf,

lies face up in the water.
Here, the fog even denies the hole.
Then sounds of breaking glass, and Lofti

sees ice thrown in sheets, shattering again on land.

At the end of an easy lope,
a muzzle smoothed from blood and honey.
The long mouth opens, pulled by lips thin and bowing.

Magnus is the bear—
spares his brother the intimate weaknesses,
knows the bones will look more
like broken sycamore branches

after just a single season.

She Was Already Root

—after Rilke

It's abominable to think of one's grandmother that way,
especially when she's alive, and we love her.
But a child sees what it says; & maybe it slips
out, & the grown-ups are ashamed for you.
So you become a dog—which always worked before.
& you know to leave the kitchen by the wide, white eggs
of their eyes, impossible to imitate without laughing.
& you know you'd better pray to God
before too much time passes. But instead you watch
a drowsy fly, heavy from hunger, decide to chase after it
with the shallow sterling bowling trophy
filled with graying green mints no one has eaten
for years.

But the fly hangs a left into the den

just as you're ready to bring the bowl up to its legs;
so you forget all about the floor ending at the hutch.
Mother's blown-glass pelicans scream for joy
and dive for the mints
bouncing off the parquet floor. & the trophy
has leapt from your hands to save itself,
spinning toward the couch like a wet galaxy.

Your mother's speed surprises you,
& she drags you down the hall
by a collar that will never be forgiven.

The bedroom buzzes with remorse.
The toys avoid your gaze.
The chameleon blends into the pulled-bark

stick, & you can tell the prayer you begin
will never make it through the shake-shingle roof.
& just as you are about to cry

the door mumbles, & your grandmother walks in
with something staining a pink paper napkin.
She rubs your puckered knees & sighs,
& you smell her diet of rose-water tea
as she kisses your cheek, & asks,
"How much of a root am I?"

Evening of the Tipped Boat and Our Resting

Last year's mound of dirt subsumes dirt
until crabgrass makes it a hill.

The yearling sheep, ears notched
in code, stand shocked among the gnats.

The crocus blooms dim.

The grass sloughs off into the sky.

I listen against your back as you sleep.
Frustrated, flies tap and leave at the windows.
I hear the house through them.

III

one two, eight nine

—elegy for James Louis Kelley

The source exchanges
past and future, allows thoughts to rise,
what eats you.

Or let's just say you met yourself
going the other way, and that's why you
insisted on leaving.

You never left the bed except for that smoke
out into a bedroom door.
Leaving everything is the trick
of dying—
a winter rain dissolves an early spring,
the living wash out the mole's midden.

The boat sinks into the yard.

Salt on the Skin Bites Like a Bug

On the night a moon danced the jig of Kali
across the tablecloths of the Coasted Crab,
between the mallets, the great inverted landscape of claws,
into my blue enameled finger bowl—
a paper bag becomes the cat and back again.

The evening had its hair,
and I was the youngest of seven guests,
with nothing to say.

An old man to my left at the large patio table
was looking at the same thing:
The cat grooming, bent in two,
until the breeze with a scent of rain
tumbled its true brown
through the trailing lights.

Its motion was elastic in the sense of a new leaf,
or like a certain place in a story he began to tell
in which a house rests where, below,
the alienated colors of decay and paloma lime
dimpled the cold fire pit.

These layers of ash and bone
used to be near a river's slow elbow.
The men spoke only here.
Their hunting silent.

Once, a boy in their party
surprised a lion, and was run down.
The panic quick, and silent.

The men buried him where the river slurries
where he had walked to cool his feet.

He paused long enough for me to think of a question:
had the boy mistaken the lion,
resting in the reeds, for rocks?

His answer was an involved spaghetti doodle
on a placemat,
tracing a walk from memory,
as if from the height of a tethered balloon.

He walks again the path with his limp,
remembering as he goes, a minor pyramid
—a box with an X—
the prison near the reeds
—concentric squares—
a great dune,
where at its crest he made uplifted breasts
brought together with dew.

They pointed the approximate way to Giza,
and would by noon
sift into the lidless eyes of a blinking god.

This man, a poor translator, loses his way
in the dialects of the river's edge—an ibis,
the thirsty jackal in the crocodile's mouth—
steering him correctly to Cairo
and to the writing of careful notebooks.

* * *

Imitating the humming sumac,
a bird beats its wings by your ear ...

How can you not hear my hunting
with winter's last smells
sealing shut the back door ...

You hoped for an orange year, and received it,

wrapped in loud prayers.
I'll skin it in your ritual way:

beginning with mouth over the navel, then
excising the one white vein, loosing
the bitter oils ...

I'll wait in the half-light of the next room,
while the budgies snap their beaks at the rain,
comforted by their say-so,

as your shadow sits
counting the mismatched cups—
a study of crazing porcelain.

Now you can imagine the moon—
the sun's jealousy

for the overturned lacquered tea bowl.

Here, the artist paints a moon in a blue sky.

The Dangers of Water, West Nile

(West Nile disease was discovered on the West Nile
of Uganda, 1937)

There are eager turns just before night—
the hum in narrow shadows
of newborns in distant cooling pools.
The winter birds stop singing
and are unable to fly.
Only the crows talk above
the Acholi crocodile hunters,
who have given up their silence
by walking with the wind.
The nearest crow is a mile away.

The river's old knowledge
crumbles below the new intelligence
that has discovered the steep beach,
clear-cut trading post,
and a forest beyond.
Large English tents re-pitched
across newly ripped green planks
wag as boxes of munitions and rifles
pass along a pivot line of men
to the wide flat-bottomed boats.
A moon rises despite the pied blue sky.

The rains stopped almost two days ago.
The clouds moved south,
leaving twitching pools of food.
The river, humped with new veins,
carries giant leafed trees.
On a fig tree, a family of monkeys
leaps straight up into the air,

each quarter revolution
of canopy, their silhouettes
a tired circling of mosquitoes.
Meanwhile, the aggregate of flies waits patiently,
on toppled, dissolving salt licks.

From the hill, the forest floor gleams black.
Trail awash, the hunters follow after
a memory of trees to the trading post.

They pause to wait for their eyes.
The canopy having thickened the night.
Above them, in the upper reaches, crows
call what these men know as the several
variations of the roosting song.

Stars wander in the water,
constellations
the men do not recognize
flicker out and arrive back
with their steps,
and one star flaps,
does not struggle as the lead man
picks up the white-breasted crow.
It acts like an old man's pet.

Within the moon shade,
the hunters watch crows float
into the English camp, the living
with beaks open, hissing
at the large catfish flushed
from their mud nests.

And the fish feed,
mouths closed on tail feathers, a wing
weakly motioning, a crow
pulling its white breast into its neck
above a flat brown head, singing
even as it disappears.

The loading has stopped.
Some men simply shoot the fish,
while others use clubs.
The Acholi walk away.
They will be the first to tell
how in two days
the stories of the world will have to change,
because, again, we lied:
birds can swim,
and the boniest fish
have become their sworn enemies.

Playing with the Ducal Hosepipe at Gotha

*We compare the Newtonian theory of colours to an old castle,
which was first constructed by its architect with youthful
precipitation; it was, however, gradually enlarged and equipped by
him according to the exigencies of time and circumstances, and
moreover was still further fortified and secured in consequence of
feuds and hostile demonstrations.*
            —*Johann Wolfgang von Goethe, Preface to the First
            Edition in* Theory of Colours

The host stands at the sweating window
surrounded by the smell
of cooling tuliped salads,
smoked duck and pickled boar,
that sigh across their silver presentation.

The Burgundian claret
in the stag theme crystal
leaves behind
thin residues of provenance.
The lit candles sputter.
Guests,
some in half silhouette, sit
frozen in positions they regret,
each, but for a lucky few,
having had to crane around
the crested powdered pompadours.

The dinner bell had been rung,
and a servant sent
for the guest of honor. Goethe
never heard the request, or he did
and ignored the summons.

He had commandeered the Moor from the stables
and was in the middle of instructing him
on how to hold a thumb
over the hose to achieve
a perfect spray of sunset.

Goethe allied with pen,
prism, and notebook, sat
on the bluing grass.
The Moor told himself there was nothing to fear
when the Duke appeared, arms slack,
at the window.
Nubs of sun flare
and will wink out in moments,
his turban the only afterglow. But

a full moon rises, and Goethe
dances the Moor around
until the spray thrums at the glass,
the ripples

reflecting back into the room
the rouge of the Duke's cheeks,
his conundrum.

Pie Chart

And God said, "Bury your dead this way:
... to the north, feet toward the south."

The churchyard plots like spilled sticks
follow the sun's path,
the comings and goings of snow geese,
and a moon's setting.

Order had to come from someplace.
The eye wants it, and it had been ages
since God demanded anything ...

At the eclipse, we admire the totality
of light that spills around the moon.
No stars appear. Our clouds seem
friendlier, the birds silent as eyes,
the sky unapologetic.

Moths wake up
and mistake the blue milk in buckets
for starlight.

From space, looking straight down
at either pole,
the moon's shadow warps away a perfect
wedge of pie. The slices equaling
more than fifty percent:
Appetites spilling over.

Later, the scooping away of
moth dust, incorporating, and kept.
No one will mention this?

The woman tells the man to bring calf's blood.
She combines the milk and blood with flour. A batter
she pours onto a blackened, round skillet.
The baked color of these cakes she makes for them
is only the beginning of another reversal
of a moon's event
fed to each other the last day of Lent.

Novena on Vectors and Pathways

Even as I smuggled into New Hampshire
a certain slick, tapered seed
from my Arizona yard,
a potential starling in a shell,
an imbroglio in the making stuck
to that tacky whip of tar
on the instep of my Oxford,

a half-finished tumbler of cranberry juice
and vodka of the night before,
left on the balustrade of the porch, fills
with yellow jackets

who quarrel within a drowning within a thirst.

The sun's heat will drive them back to their jobs,
and then I'll take the glass inside,
pour the dead and near dead down the drain.
But until then, I watch them writhe and battle
as men might do

over a woman perhaps,
or for a job at a factory or mine.

Over breakfast this morning,
a scholar, a woman of novice beauty,
sporting a coif, Medusa-cut,
tells me she is writing a book on the invasive species,

exotics, planted or released.

So, little seed, what are you?

If I toss you out the back door
will you send tendrils into the lodge pole pines
to bloom, releasing
the most edible scent the deer have ever smelled,

so all they do is stand, craning into the boughs,
hooves cowed to the spicy bark?

Perhaps, you will simply stay a seed, choosing
seediness as your life,

remaining a volunteer, potential paperweight
for ants, abiding the nighttime of tunnels,
until, at last, the final instruction comes,

and you sprout, the first color
along a gray and buckled shore.

The Late Evangel of the Whale Fjord

Suspicion is a form of imagination
but love is, too ....
          —Delmore Schwartz

The only news I have is that the bay whined for two years
and the clouds noted the bluffs.
And all the while I was walking home to you
again, to your father's estate, up
to the "parapet,"
as he gazed down at the summer
administered
across the diligent but angry swirls

of his fragile putting green.

I have a cat I named after him.

Your father was always like the grass roof I repaired:
clumsy but also a success. Like the time
he held out a cruelly
dry hand, and said, "Let's not say goodbye. Let's
just say *arrivederci*." I laughed.

Took his hand, and somehow you wound up in Rome.

Like an idiot in a wheat field, this place, at first,
troubled me, provided no flourishes
except for a flock of feral hens.
No one lives along the hay anymore

but everything has been named—there's
a pitted stone you could kick
that's called Hjalti's Stone,

because this man, an Irish shepherd, a Viking
slave, was chopped down there,
even while he was being hailed—
feuds seldom begin more dramatically.

Those settlers didn't come here to live in peace.
So let's just agree that I am the consanguinean
and cognate, a late example
you might say, scribbling out
my revenge ...

But mischief never agrees to my terms.
Each time I compose this letter,
you become more abstract,
and even now, all I'm addressing is your left
eye, green with hazel tatters. Just like,
I'm hoping, your father's lawn, spotted now
with gorse. Him suffering

despite your attentions.

Monsters Don't Always Have Beaks

after a painting by Odd Nerdrum

So many things I want to tell you
no one outside of the family knows:
like the afternoon the volcano, *Hekla*,
steamed and stirred.

As luck has it,
I'm sitting in the clover, staring at her
with all the eyes grown out of my loneliness,
when she releases a papal smoke,
stuttered and white.

These clouds circle over me
as my nose splits open
and out comes a blue eye.

My body spouts tentacles—
at their ends,
open eyes.

Hekla erupts, draws lightning
to her mouth.

These stalks of blue curl over me
into a wave—
eyes, like dogs' ears, pointing toward the source of

drumming that startles the horses
to the furthest fence, where they run
its length of bones,
beseeching the dropping sky.

Calmly,
with her rented sack,
she collects their cries.

IV

Delirium at the Prado

The fleur-de-lis of the iron fences slump in a friendly way. Tourists fill the burn wards. In Madrid, swimming pools turn to acid—robin's-egg blue no child can resist. The crops rattle as the dew dries again. The deer are done with them. The mountains send off rocks to bounce, making their rough noises out of loneliness. A whole room of skeletons where no creature has been spared the wire. And then the jars. How can a world fit into a jar without the once clear waters yellowing? The solution has changed into the same color Velasquez chose as royal sunlight for room after room hung with tapestry. He painted the prince's dwarf under a gray, cloudy sky—the color of worked wire and spiderwort. Off of the feathers and pelts, bubbles of my confusion form in the summer heat. The skeletons forget their poses. The foxes crouch, waiting for the right moment.

The City's in a Fever and I Follow in, Me: El Rubio

Throughout the Old Quarter gypsies want me to pose, paint my slapdash life on top of theirs across Clorox triptychs or on whatever tin can was lying around. More than that they touch my hair, then pure with a comet's dust. So I take up wearing my father's black fedora, emphasizing the faux bamboo cane and my limp. Yet, they saw through the disguise. Poor *El Rubio*, they said, so golden and lame. His pain is our itch.

Something You Need to Know about Avondale

Christmas Eve and a drunken moth is trying to come on to an embalmed snowflake while shouting at a string of blue Christmas lights about some war or another and friends dead in their jobs, when he spies me watching him from the topiary of a sperm whale battling a colossus squid. "Hey, hey, hey, Botany 500 boy, is it that bad? *That* bad?" I stiffen into a cigarette, because I remember what all Latin School pupils have drilled into them: Plod the Lesser's tombstone epitaph, *Of all the types of soothsayers, the drunk's guess is as good as any.* "Kid, what's your name?" Mack, I say. "Okay, Jake, listen. There's something you need to know before the world ends. Tim, the world ends when you end, *verstanze*?" And I swear, I saw the squid nod, as it was slurped into the belly of myrtle.

Prayer Salts

Throughout my night's muttering and the moon's whir, I pray to the gods of wild bees, for daily discoveries that must happen. And for the in-between times, when noon stops breathing, and drones thrum at doors, to keep honey from flowing, waiting eggs white, the queen in her glistening. Others fly to brown pools, fill mouths with grit, and maybe wrap it on a back leg. The dribble will soak into the paper house, slowly form a shell, and pull the world from its paste.

I once saw a bee on a rose petal throb like a star. I knew then that dying to a bee was just another thought of doing. And then it curls. Good work done. The hairs on my legs are glued with prayer salts, and the breeze has tied them.

Visitation of the Chemotherapy Angel

1.
The phenomenon of a waking dream came while the world around me slept like a pigeon in its fluff. A pearl, pelt luminescence, short, without traits, a human shape: Requisition of my selfish prayers. *Great is the wealth within you*, its gesture, not of embrace, but forbearance. *I take you for what you are, not less*, palms upward, where the unsubstantiated mind rests.

This angel is the diminutive, bald guardian of the bad bowler who tries, of the starving weed among the overwhelming growth. It steps toward me. I am propped on an elbow. Just moments before, in dream, I stood at the back door, before a hound with a savage human face, waiting, like the pet, to be let in.

In the next room, the patient sleeps off the weariness of short, wakeful moments of previous days. It's not long before his one lung stops. I return the gesture with my own: palm thrust—refusal of mercy.

2.
In the notebooks of the illness are studies of static lines, cribs for bridges between here and there, which after the patient's death, dissolve like a noisy tree of birds. The first and last pages somehow remain.

> "What we fear is the dead awakening once we've buried them. Even a loved pet we keep in a box with a towel overnight. It is a wallet too big for the back pocket. What's valuable and exposed. Its loss is a note on a napkin. The writing keeps for lack of air. The broken fibers are worm tracks. Daily, you chase a woodpecker from the spine, not knowing why."

> "God mirrors us, even in our pain."

V

Sniper's-nest, Iceland, Circa 1941

Today the river was more than the mountain,
horizon diminished by the house,
the open graves should fit in her pockets.
Her uncles' hands keep Runa from roaring
like the bee among the offerings.

She feels her hunger rise ...

She knew death was the nutrient,
lungs of low tide a complete thought.
The waves return in the gusts' arms,
just as the moon moves slowly at incredible speed.
A fact she observed by dissolving
first as the loved child
and then as a lonely woman.

More dying and no witness.

An arctic fox doesn't see
death when chasing down a duck,
or when it cinches the windpipe ...
So dying is not witnessed
as the moving
of life away from life,
but is suddenness
the fox knows
in the mouth.

This moment of intuition has its living companion.
It is a moment
free of sheep, wind, and water.

And Runa holds the cup of water

to her uncle's lips. It reflects itself, what wasn't
taken in.

Nebuchadnezzar, son of Nebuchadnezzar,
the last of two brothers,
her uncles,
her mother's brothers who raised her,

has died in the hay loft from an attack
of asthma.

Down the bay on a strip of sea cobbles
growing fine,
the whale lies breathing.

These strandings happen at night,
a fact of her waking.

She imagines it, like her friend,
leaving the sea for the bay,
swimming through dark reflections
cast on wintry black water
to the mouth of the fjord
that widens.

She thinks it must be that

the waters never narrow, *is what
they see.*

* * *

She felt alone, but then the postcard arrived,

a silhouette
in a room where ivory is cured like wood.
Exhausted, the living cells
simplify. The old men called it *cooling*.

On the postcard is a painting of Baltimore's harbor,
failing stars fill the sky, and the handwritten note,
we live near here
across the white border circled in a child's blue cloud.
Its final loop leads out into the picture
across the roofs along the wharf,
ending in a vacant field.

She tries to imagine a sky like that,
under which her daughter's house sits.
She hopes it isn't far from a store.
She leans the picture against the sugar bowl.

        * * *

It seems my life began with the same dream:
waking from speed,
emerging from a place of no stars.

I would open my eyes before
the momentum arrived, the dark room
buzzing, my eyes repeating light.

I would notice a faint smell of liquor,
like opening a box with moldy bread,
a loaf slowly displacing space.

I never drink because of those dreams,

and imagine speed as a comet,
suspended within this black bread
I tear apart for chickens.

The comet means my end
and is as real
as crocuses blooming in old snow.
This example is my patience and my work—
I move my small garden
to the windless side of the house:

After years of only believing in sun,
the tulip buds now shred against us.

Now, I accept   ♦
never seeing their reflections on the windows,
relive the years of burying cod heads,
sift the subtle bones
—bloodworms curling from my hands.

The pitchfork brings up shells,
or shapes of shells, mineralized
they crumble in the air,

reminding me of waves capping
over bows, returning to a color
never mistaken for white.

I have lacquered some of the shells—
some open, some sealed.
They remind me of how I've changed,

how one day,
I will dare to keep my eyes
and follow the comet's path up
and through my chest.

I could tell you when.

        * * *

She sits in her future and waits for the past
to wake up. They move together,
creating her, the daughter,
and her routine, at evening …

Yet Runa's daughter could never understand
how her mother would wake from the past,
how she must say where she has been
without repeating.
How when the teakettle blew
Runa was opening a door
while her daughter stood before
her pouring the water for the tea,
and two British officers,
one, the man who would be the daughter's father,
stood by a motorcycle smiling—the other
wringing his hands.

The officers were surveying the coast for safe harbors,
and they spoke to her as if she knew about the war.
They spoke to her as if they could explain
why that morning the ground-nesting birds

flew from their bevies: some landing
like a heartbeat in an egg,
some tapping as long knuckles along the house.

       * * *

The moss has spent lifetimes moving across a field,
ready to overturn its cold water,
loose in its waves,
except here where the wind brings grit.
The bloodwort holds the sod
even in its browning.

The moss will lose to the shoehorn grass—

its trumpets of fungi, pointing
their sex toward the sea.

Like the orange poppies, they burst
with the unlikeliest breeze.
These burnt poppies had claimed the dry hillocks,
slowing the melt water
as it cuts a road.

Lupine own the road.
Their roots can't hold this stain
that leeches an angry skin,

her dark embroidery of house

sewn with cloth not yarn,
the threads frayed,

one filament of sun that never reaches ground.
These lines formed her dead friend's mouth—
a haystack,
next to an impossible hairdo of oak.

Fence posts of driftwood,
barbwire strung,
and absent of birds.
A noise like shore birds
takes its time on the wind.
It could be the mob gathering,
the gray slump of the whale.

Their tall hats have upset the pipers.

These men slaughtered the chickens,
left them for Runa to bury ...

She struggles through root and simple dirt,
tearing cloth beyond the haystack.

The turf slides from the brindled mass.

Morning eggs are in the drying timothy,
dandelions on the roof,
a wisp of coal fire ending the day ...

A house among the rusting talus.
Ochre and green hems tire
of shadows in the cliffs.
Emptiness,

with the sea.

* * *

Runa waits with a nervous cigarette
for visitors who use their own doors.
Her daughter plays with God's own
last name, her blood of grasses and aching,
whose presence she felt in the dream
selecting a hat among so many hats.

Runa finally chose the washed-out blues
of intimacy.

She invented the austerity of one teacup,
squeezing with a spoon the brown leaves
of second-hand news.

Her mind fills with hungry birds

as she circles the cup three times
over her head

and rests its surprised mouth
on the spoon to dry.

Her friend reads the stains like an argument
—affliction of age and knowing:

Just as you may not believe
the thrush's call a song
suited to the rising form, so

the length of its beak
balances against a persistent
brown—you may just as well call it
the barking of a titmouse,
perched on his single note of waiting.

Your man knows where to find you.

   * * *

Runa sits before the tall border grass—
invisible
to the sheep who have slipped
below the fence
to feed after the fresh mowing.
Ripping is a movement of the head
they'll do all their lives,
until they starve—
teeth stained green, even after boiling,
their gentle slopes of uselessness.

In a warped wooden kitchen spoon
Runa discovers an even gaze of burl,
a woman's face, with a halo exact as the dew claws of dog.
She, at times, rubs these rays with pollen,
and takes them to the sheep slough between the fields
to look out over the fulmars who forgot their eggs,
to protect the ducks from foxes' song,
to ensure the boulders staying put, to give
strength to the reed grass rope
she wove into embraces …

She comes to this place—
away from the clocked silence of the house,
where she sat in the chair
turning the blunt whale tooth
her father saved.
A tooth without a story, he said.

Ripped from the jaw, the thick
root-stem flowers.

She looks for its secret

where there is depth—
a view.

Within the grain
she sees the suggestion of rufus
from out at sea,
the sky crackling in amber glow,
the seabed bent by a swell, the water
gathering speed to itself.

Runa, waiting on the shore.
The tidal pool withdraws.
She welcomes the waves
and the sound of a difficult bell.

* * *

Holding the red end of an oversized book,
while her grandson, his mouth around her wrist—
the puma's sawtooth bite—

growls with pleasure,
she says, pointing to the page,
You are the good cat.

She is the child of his language,
who can awake to a smell of fish
and confuse it with birdsong outside.

She turns the page as he chants
dead, dead, dead.
The doe's eye is what she sees,
her own fear repeated,
in his picture book of meat-eaters.

The last page has no prey.
A brown mouse hunches before a juniper berry
swelling in a drying caribou patty.

There is no tree line here,

only familiar rock and moss,
and ground-creeping juniper ...

She wants to tell him the berries take
years to ripen, except when the wax
is thinned through the stomachs of the herd.

She wants to say that the picture
is drawn from a south view, since
the caribou stand to the left of the rocks.

No dead, she says,

but the boy points to a darkened horn
in the eastern sky—
its distance removes any color
just as the poppies and lupine
on the mountain slopes turn
into the knurl of peaks.

The mouse is about to lose itself
to its meal.

This hesitant moment
its prelude and habit.

The boy grabs, then slams the book shut.
Runa doesn't blink, yet the room
vanishes.

On the endcover,
the falcon stands on its catch.

When her vision returns, she is looking
into the eyes of Manni,
and realizes she is laughing.

But she looks to the berry,
its tourmaline surface
changing with the sun's path
to a bruise.

Not only distance, but time,
collapses, and Runa herself—
the thoughts that have always been

the warm hand in hers,
of equal heat, are gone.

She knows the falcon *screech*
and the mouse *squeak*,
simultaneously gone,
like a bee lost in the nap
of a fresh-cut
cliff rose.

NOTES

The title *Skeletons of Spirits* is the English translation of "Andans Beingrind," the title of a metal sculpture made in 1961 by Icelandic sculptor Sigurjón Ólafsson (1908 – 1982).

The title of the poem "She Was Already Root," is a line from Marie Rilke's poem "Orpheus, Eurydice, Hermes," translated by Stephen Mitchell in *Ahead of All Parting: The Selected Poetry and Prose of Rainer Maria Rilke* (New York: The Modern Library, 1995).

"Sniper's-nest, Iceland, circa 1941" is dedicated to my mother, Áslaug Hermanníusdóttir Burawa, who, in the great tradition of Icelanders, taught me all the history she knows.